I0759746

The Constellation Ursa Minor

LISA OWINGS

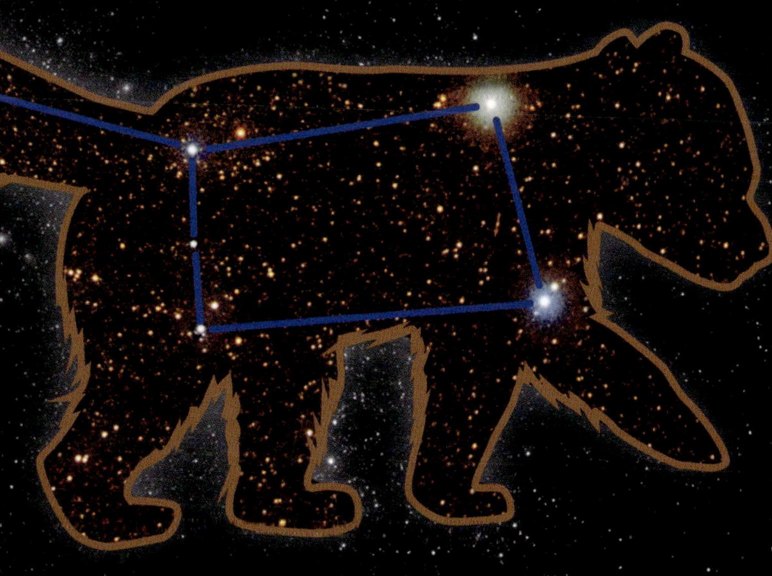

Published by The Child's World®
800-599-READ • www.childsworld.com

Photography Credits
Photographs ©: iStockphoto, cover (illustration), 1 (illustration), 2 (illustration), 10 (illustration), 15 (Miletus), 15 (Thales); E. Slawik/NSF/AURA/M. Zaman/NOIRLab, cover (constellation), 1 (constellation), 2 (constellation), 10 (constellation); Shutterstock Images, cover (background), 1 (background), 2–3, 5, 7, 8, 19, 24 (background), 24 (gods), 27 (wolf), 27 (coyote); N. Evans/H. Bond/NASA/ESA/Hubble, 9; Giuseppe Donatiello/Flickr, 13 (top); NASA, 13 (bottom); Sidney Hall/Library of Congress, 16; Metropolitan Museum of Art, 21; Gabriela Insuratelu/Shutterstock Images, 22; Jim Cumming/Shutterstock Images, 27 (fox); Eric Isselee/Shutterstock Images, 27 (dogs); Alan Dyer/VWPics/AP Images, 29; Design elements from Shutterstock Images

ISBN Information
9781503875845 (Reinforced Library Binding)
9781503876262 (Portable Document Format)
9781503876880 (Online Multi-user eBook)
9781503877382 (Electronic Publication)

LCCN 2025938271

Printed in the United States of America

ABOUT THE AUTHOR

Lisa Owings has a degree in English and creative writing from the University of Minnesota. She has written and edited a wide variety of educational books for young people. Lisa lives in Andover, Minnesota, where Ursa Minor is in the sky every night.

Page 15 of this book refers to the country of Turkey. The US State Department and United Nations have recognized the spelling change *Türkiye* in formal contexts to better represent the Turkish language. In this book, the more familiar anglicized name is used to ensure that place names and geography are recognizable to all readers.

TABLE OF CONTENTS

CHAPTER ONE

The Constellation Ursa Minor

People have long watched the movements of stars. The stars wheel across the sky. They rise and set each night. They move through the seasons of the year, too. As people watch the sky, Earth spins on its axis. That is why the Sun seems to rise and set. It is why the stars seem to circle the heavens. For centuries, one star has held a special place in the northern sky. It shines almost directly above the axis at the North Pole. Because of this, the star never seems to move. This star is called Polaris, or the North Star. Polaris and the stars around it form the constellation Ursa Minor, the Little Bear.

The other stars in the night sky circle around Polaris, which does not seem to move.

Only a small fraction of the stars in the universe are visible from Earth. They form bright patterns in the night sky. For **ancient** stargazers, some groups of stars stood out more than others. Since long ago, people have traced pictures in these stars. They told stories about the pictures. These groups of stars are called constellations. Today, there are 88 constellations. The Greco-Roman **astronomer** Ptolemy (TAH-luh-mee) wrote about the first 48 almost 2,000 years ago. Most of these are included in the modern constellations. Others were added later. The entire sky is split into 88 divisions. Everything in the night sky belongs to one of the constellations.

It is easy to think of stars as tiny lights. But they are actually giant, fiery balls of gas. They can burn for billions of years. The closest star to Earth is the Sun. It is 93 million miles (150 million km) away. There are billions of stars in the night sky. Many are hundreds of times bigger and brighter than the Sun. And most are trillions of miles farther away.

Earth's Sun is a star.

Polaris is the most important star in Ursa Minor. It lights the tip of the Little Bear's tail. Polaris serves as a bright **compass** in northern skies. Countless sailors have relied on it to keep their ships on course.

Polaris has not always held its unique position. Like a top, Earth wobbles as it spins. Unlike a top, it wobbles very slowly. Since long ago, the North Pole has been tipped toward Polaris. But someday Earth will slowly wobble away again. Then a different star will take Polaris's place above the pole.

Earth spins on its axis as it moves around the Sun. Polaris sits above the axis, which is why it does not appear to move.

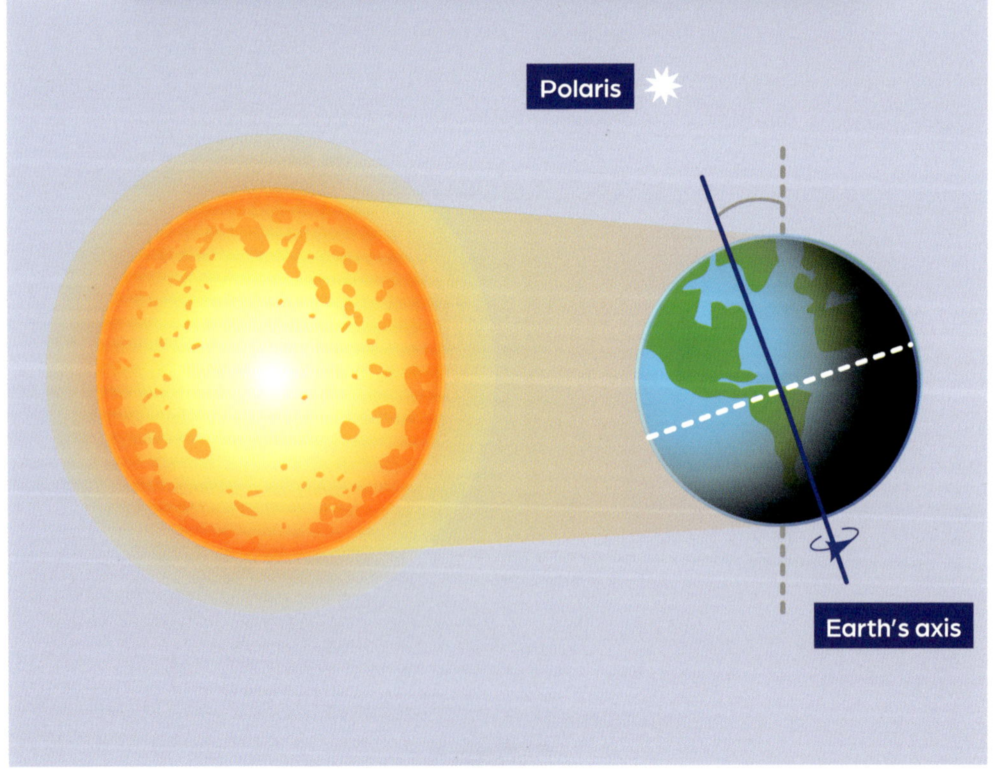

A TRIPLE STAR

Polaris is not alone at the top of the world. It is part of a system of three stars. One of its smaller companions is relatively easy to spot. This is Polaris B. The other, Polaris Ab, is so close to Polaris that it is almost impossible to see. Only extremely powerful telescopes such as the **Hubble Space Telescope** can separate Polaris Ab from Polaris.

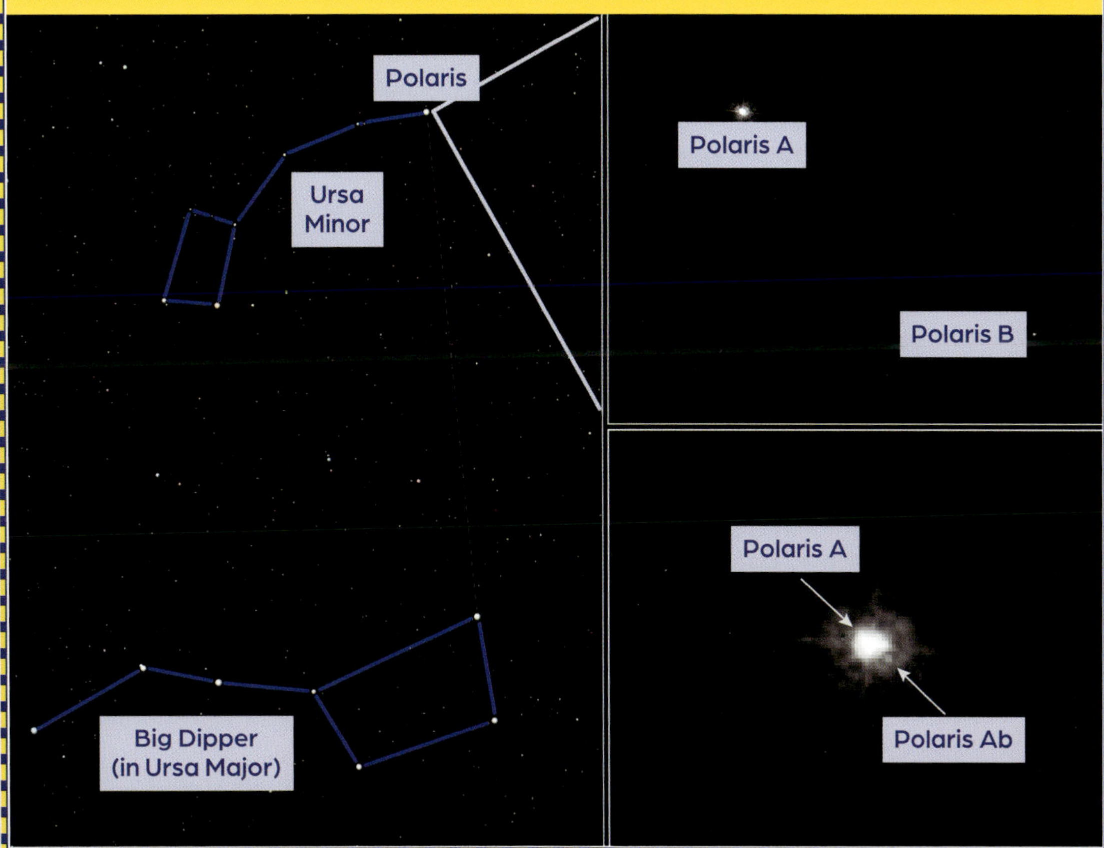

The Greek myths about Ursa Minor explain its long tail. Real bears have short tails.

The seven brightest stars of Ursa Minor form the Little Dipper. This is an asterism. Asterisms are groups of stars that are not official constellations. The Little Dipper has a similar shape to the nearby Big Dipper. The Big Dipper is an asterism that is part of Ursa Major, the Great Bear. The Little Dipper's handle is Ursa Minor's tail. Its bowl is the Little Bear's body.

Polaris is not the brightest star in the sky. But it is the brightest star in Ursa Minor. It forms the end of the bear's tail. Pherkad and Kochab are the brightest stars in Ursa Minor's body. Kochab is almost as bright as Polaris.

The Little Dipper and Ursa Minor have mostly the same stars. But 24 Ursae Minoris and 18 Ursae Minoris are not part of the Little Dipper. This is what makes the Little Dipper an asterism.

Constellations contain more than just stars. They also contain deep-sky objects such as **galaxies**. Ursa Minor Dwarf is a galaxy in Ursa Minor. It is a satellite galaxy to the Milky Way, Earth's galaxy. Satellite galaxies **orbit** larger galaxies.

Dwarf galaxies do not always have a clear structure as seen in other galaxies.

CHAPTER TWO

THE ORIGIN OF THE MYTH

Thousands of years ago, the Phoenicians and the Greeks sailed wooden ships over the Mediterranean Sea. These sailors were skilled at finding their way on ocean waters. They used the stars to guide them. They knew the stars showed them the way north. If they did not know which stars to steer by, their ships would be lost.

Greek sailors relied on Ursa Major. Its stars were bright and easy to see. But Phoenicians used Ursa Minor. Its stars were harder to see. But they moved in a tighter circle around the North Pole. That meant they were a more exact compass. The astronomer Thales (THAY-leez) knew of the constellation that guided Phoenician sailors. Stories say Thales taught the Greeks about Ursa Minor around 600 BC. He suggested that sailors steer by this smaller group of stars. To this day, Ursa Minor and the star Polaris are known as the markers of true north.

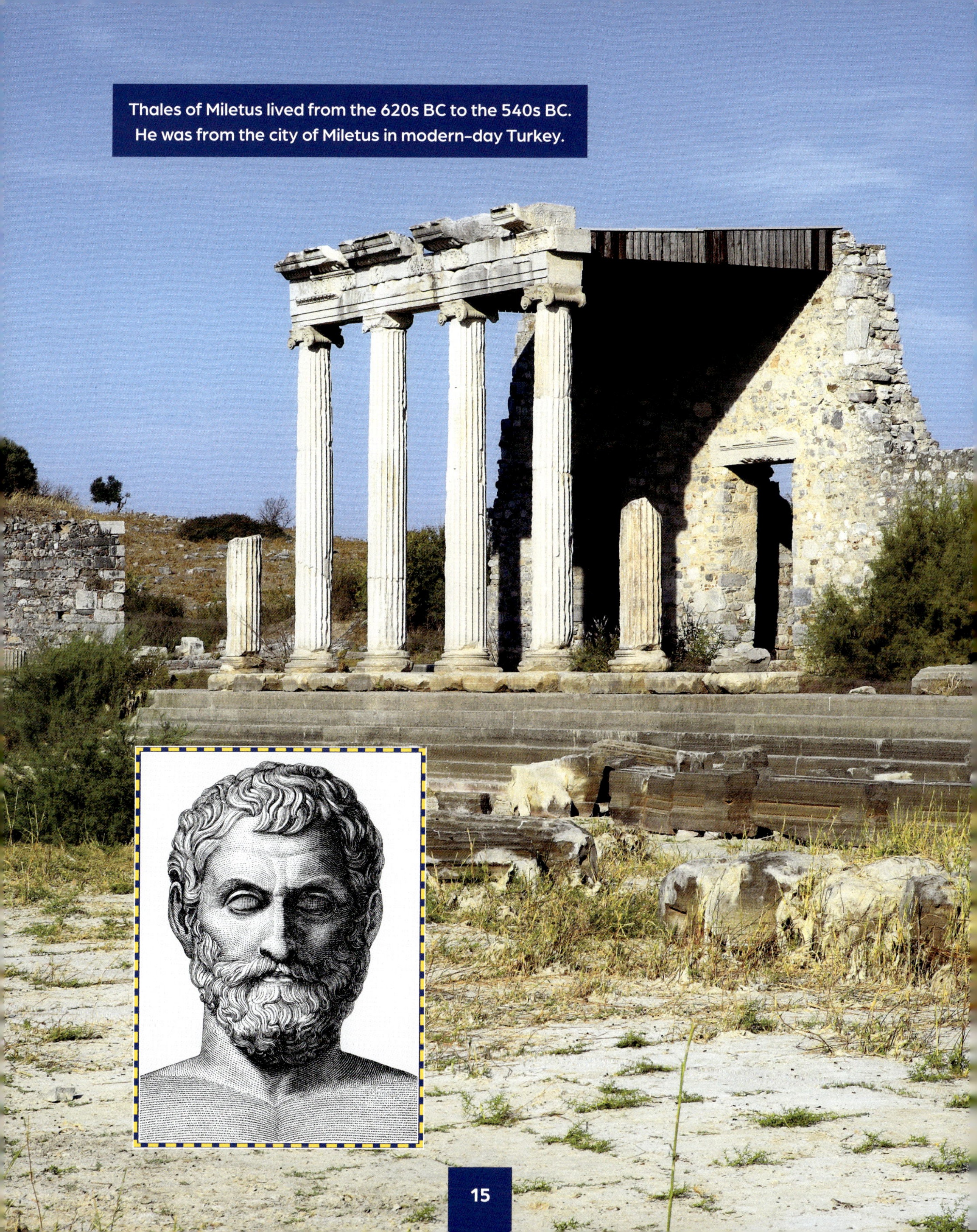

Thales of Miletus lived from the 620s BC to the 540s BC. He was from the city of Miletus in modern-day Turkey.

DRACO

Ursa Minor is nestled close to another constellation. The body of the star-dragon Draco curves around the Little Bear. At one time, the stars of Ursa Minor may have been seen as Draco's wings. But Ursa Minor eventually became its own constellation.

The ancient Greeks welcomed this new constellation. By around 300 BC, they fit it into their stories about Ursa Major. The Greek poet Aratus said the two bears in the sky were from the island of Crete. They had cared for the god Zeus when he was an infant. Many versions of this story are told today.

CHAPTER THREE

The Story of Ursa Minor

In the earliest days of the world, Gaia (GY-uh) and Ouranos (OO-ran-ohss) had many children. Gaia was the goddess of the Earth. Ouranos was the god of the sky. Their children were powerful gods and goddesses called Titans. Cronus was the youngest.

Ouranos and Gaia were fighting. Gaia encouraged her children to defeat Ouranos. They did, and Cronus became king. He married Rhea. Soon they were expecting a child.

Rhea was happy. But Cronus was not. He had replaced his father as king. His parents told him that one day, one of his children would do the same to him. The mighty Cronus was filled with fear. He hatched a terrible plan to hold on to his power.

Cronus did not want to give up his power.

As soon as Rhea gave birth, Cronus tore the infant from her arms. Then he swallowed the newborn child! Rhea could not believe what her husband had done. Her heart broke for her lost child. Rhea had more children. But her husband swallowed every single one.

After Cronus had eaten five of her children, Rhea became pregnant again. She could not bear to lose another child. She begged Gaia and Ouranos to help her. They told her exactly what to do.

Rhea followed their advice. When it came time for her to give birth, she went to the island of Crete. There she secretly gave birth to a son. She called him Zeus. Gaia took the child. She hid him in a dark mountain cave. Two goddesses, Ida and Adrasteia, lived nearby. They agreed to care for the young god.

Rhea was glad her son was safe. Now she had to fool her husband. She found a heavy stone. She wrapped a soft blanket around it. She cradled the stone in her arms like a baby. Then she went to see her husband. As Rhea hoped, Cronus mistook the bundle for his son. He snatched up the stone and swallowed it whole.

Rhea tricked Cronus into eating a rock instead of their child Zeus.

Visitors to the island of Crete can visit the cave some people say was the birthplace of Zeus. It is known as Dikteon Andron, the Cave of Zeus, or Psychro Cave.

Inside the cave on Crete, Ida and Adrasteia looked after Zeus. They fed him golden honey. A goat offered him her milk. When it was time to sleep, the women rocked Zeus in a golden cradle. Adrasteia made a pretty toy for him. It was a golden ball. Zeus loved to throw it in the air. A trail of light followed the ball wherever it went. **Warriors** stood guard outside the cave. They shouted and beat their shields with their spears. The noise kept Zeus's cries from reaching Cronus's ears.

(From left) Hestia, Poseidon, Zeus, Hera, Demeter, and Hades were the first six of the Olympian gods. There were 12 total.

Zeus grew up quickly on the island of Crete. He was furious when he learned what his father had done. But Gaia knew a way to get **revenge**. She made Cronus feel sick. Suddenly, he vomited up a heavy stone. Then, one by one, he threw up each of Zeus's brothers and sisters. The gods Poseidon and Hades came first. The goddesses Hera, Demeter, and Hestia followed.

Zeus's **siblings** were happy to be free. They joined him in a battle against Cronus and the other Titans. After ten long years, Zeus and his followers won the war. They defeated the monstrous Cronus. Zeus became king of the gods, just as Gaia and Ouranos had said.

With a thunderbolt in hand, Zeus ruled the skies. But he never forgot the goddesses who were like mothers to him. Ida and Adrasteia had saved his life. Zeus wanted to honor them. Giving them the shape of mighty bears, he swung them by their tails into the sky. That is why their tails are so long. Adrasteia became the Great Bear. The Little Bear was Ida.

CALLISTO

Some Greeks told a very different story about Ursa Minor. This story was about a beautiful hunter named Callisto. She and Zeus had a son named Arcas. Callisto was turned into a bear. Zeus turned Arcas into a bear, too. Then he took both bears by their tails and swung them into the sky. They became the Great and Little Bears.

CHAPTER FOUR

The Myth of Ursa Minor in Other Cultures

The stars around the North Pole have always seemed to rule the heavens. People often connected them to gods or kings. Chinese astronomers saw the palace of an **emperor**. In Norse mythology, the Big and Little Dippers were **chariots**. Ursa Minor was *Kvennavagn*, the Woman's Chariot, driven by the goddess Freya. Polaris was a jewel at the end of a spike. Earth rotated around it.

Native American peoples tell stories of the stars, too. The Ojibwe see Ursa Minor as *Maang*, the Loon. Loons are seen as messengers and leaders. They go between water and land. The Cree know Ursa Minor as *Atima Atchakosuk*, the Dog Stars. Long ago, there were no dogs. There were only their wild **ancestors**. These were wolves, coyotes, and foxes. The animals were worried. They thought humans needed an animal companion. The animals sent puppies in all four directions.

These puppies became today's dogs. The Creator honored the wild animals by placing them in the stars. Polaris is the Wolf Star. Then come the Coyote Star and Fox Star. The remaining four stars are the puppies.

Wolves, coyotes, foxes, and dogs are all part of the Canidae family.

CHAPTER FIVE

How to Find Ursa Minor in the Sky

Ursa Minor is a small, faint constellation. The best way to find it is to look for Polaris. The Big Dipper can be used as a guide. This asterism is brighter. Find the two stars of the dipper's bowl that are farthest from the handle. These stars are called the Pointers. Draw an imaginary line from the star at the bottom of the bowl through the one at the top. The next bright star the line crosses will be Polaris. After finding the tip of the Little Bear's tail, look for Pherkad and Kochab. If it is clear enough, the other dimmer stars will come into view.

Ursa Minor is always high in the northern sky. It seems to swing around the pole by its tail. The Little Bear's body hangs lowest in winter. It swings high above the pole in summer. People who look at the Little Bear can always find their way.

GUARDIANS OF THE POLE

The stars Pherkad and Kochab are called the Guardians of the Pole. They spend their nights marching around Polaris, seeming to keep watch. Ancient Arabs had another name for these two stars. They called them the Two Calves. The calves stayed close to their mother, Polaris.

GLOSSARY

ancestors (AN-sess-turz) Ancestors are family members from long ago. Wolves, coyotes, and foxes are all ancestors of modern dogs.

ancient (AYN-shunt) Something that is ancient is very old or belongs to times long ago. Ancient sailors used Polaris as a guide when sailing.

astronomer (uh-STRAW-nuh-mur) An astronomer is a scientist who studies stars and other objects in space. Ptolemy was an astronomer who wrote about constellations.

chariots (CHAYR-ee-uhtz) Chariots are small vehicles pulled by horses. In Norse mythology, Ursa Minor is Freya's chariot.

compass (KUM-puss) A compass is a tool that always points north and is used to help people find their way. Ursa Minor served as a compass for ancient sailors.

emperor (EM-per-er) An emperor is a ruler. Chinese astronomers saw Ursa Minor as an emperor's palace.

galaxies (GAL-uhk-seez) Galaxies are groups of dust, gases, and billions of stars held together by gravity. The Milky Way is one of many galaxies.

Hubble Space Telescope (HUB-uhl SPAYS TELL-uh-skohp) The Hubble Space Telescope is a large telescope in space that can take pictures. The Hubble Space Telescope can separate Polaris and Polaris Ab.

orbit (OR-bit) To orbit an object is to move in a rounded path around it. Satellite galaxies orbit larger galaxies.

revenge (ruh-VEHNJ) Revenge is getting back at someone for something bad they did. Zeus took revenge on Cronus for eating Zeus's siblings.

siblings (SIH-blingz) Siblings are people who share a parent or parents, such as brothers and sisters. Zeus rescued his siblings from their father's stomach.

warriors (WOR-ee-uhrz) Warriors are soldiers. Warriors made noise to protect Zeus from Cronus.

FAST FACTS

- Constellations are groupings of stars in the sky that form pictures. Stars are glowing balls of gas throughout the universe. The Sun is a star.
- The constellation Ursa Minor is the Little Bear. Polaris, the North Star, marks the tip of its tail. This star points north and does not appear to move in the night sky.
- Ursa Minor contains an asterism called the Little Dipper.
- Phoenicians used Ursa Minor as a guide when they sailed. The astronomer Thales is said to have introduced the constellation to the Greeks.
- In Greek mythology, Ursa Minor and Ursa Major were put into the sky together. Zeus swung the bears into the sky, which is why their tails are so long.
- In one Greek story, two goddesses saved Zeus from his murderous father. Zeus honored the goddesses by placing them into the stars.
- Other cultures see Ursa Minor as a chariot, a loon, or dogs.
- Ursa Minor is always in the sky in the north.

ONE STRIDE FURTHER

- This book tells many stories about Ursa Minor. Which story is your favorite? Why?
- Why do you think Zeus chose bears to honor Ida and Adrasteia?
- Try finding Polaris in the night sky. What shapes would you create from the stars around it? Are they similar to Ursa Minor, or are they different?

FIND OUT MORE

IN THE LIBRARY

Bullard, Lisa. *Auroras*. Parker, CO: The Child's World, 2025.

Lock, Deborah. *Greek Myths*. New York, NY: DK Publishing, 2023.

Owings, Lisa. *The Constellation Ursa Major*. Parker, CO: The Child's World, 2026.

ON THE WEB

Visit our website for links about Ursa Minor:

childsworld.com/links

Note to Parents, Caregivers, Teachers, and Librarians: We routinely verify our web links to make sure they are safe and active sites. So encourage your readers to check them out!

INDEX